6/02

22.90

JOHN GLENN'S
RETURN TO SPACE

GREG VOGT

The Millbrook Press
Brookfield, Connecticut

Cover photographs courtesy of NASA

Photographs courtesy of NASA: pp. 4 (both), 13, 14, 16, 17, 20, 24, 27, 28, 34, 41, 42, 44, 46, 48 (both), 51, 53, 59, 61; UPI/Corbis-Bettmann: p. 32; AP/Wide World Photos: p. 37; Corbis: p. 56.

Published by The Millbrook Press, Inc.
2 Old New Milford Road, Brookfield, CT   06804
www.millbrookpress.com

Library of Congress Cataloging-in-Publication Data
Vogt, Gregory.
John Glenn's return to space / Gregory Vogt.
p. cm.
Includes bibliographical references and index.
Summary: Details astronaut John Glenn's second flight
into space in 1998 and contrasts it with his first flight in 1962,
discussing training, equipment, and responsibilities.
ISBN 0-7613-1614-0 (lib. bdg.)
1. Space flights—Juvenile literature. 2. Glenn, John, 1921–
—Journeys—Juvenile literature. 3. Space shuttles—Juvenile
literature. 4. Astronauts—United States—Juvenile literature.
[1. Space flights. 2. Space shuttles. 3. Astronautics. 4. Glenn,
John, 1921– 5. Astronauts.] 1. Title.
TL793.V56   2000
629.45'0092—dc21   00-020768

CONTENTS

John Glenn before his historic journey into space in 1962 (above) and ready for a repeat performance in 1998 (right)

INTRODUCTION

Two events, separated by nearly thirty-six years, linked one man and created space history. As a young man, John H. Glenn Jr. was a military pilot and an astronaut. In his middle years, he became a U.S. senator from Ohio and a presidential candidate. At age seventy-seven, Glenn became an astronaut again and returned to space. Millions of people from around the world, especially older people, cheered him in his second journey through outer space. The cheering was something Glenn was used to. It had happened before.

In the 1950s, when the world was still recovering from World War II and the Korean War, the frontier was outer space. Every generation has had a frontier. For some, it was the icy poles of Earth, the next mountain range, or the vast expanse of oceans. For the generation of the 1950s, the frontier was above Earth's atmosphere. Outer space was more

difficult to reach than any other frontier and more dangerous. Exposure of an unprotected human to outer space would lead to a certain and excruciating death in less than 30 seconds. Going into outer space was not like flying an airplane in which propellers or jet engines could push you along and wings would hold you aloft. Traveling through space required the brute force of rocket engines, the delicate science of orbital dynamics, and environments sealed inside spaceships.

Before October 1957 rocket technology was crude. Using improved versions of rockets first developed for warfare, reaching outer space was possible but staying there was another matter. You not only had to reach space, some 100 miles (160 kilometers) above Earth's surface, but you also had to be traveling at a speed of some 17,600 miles (28,300 kilometers) per hour parallel to the ground to stay there. In a short time your rocket fuel would be exhausted. If you were not going fast enough and in the right direction, you would plunge back into Earth's atmosphere and burn up in the heat generated by the friction with the air. Too fast and you would spiral out into deep space, never to return. Just fast enough and in the right direction would permit you to coast around Earth. The path of your fall would match the shape of Earth. Scientists call this path an orbit. It was a good concept but yet to be achieved.

There was tension around the world as to which nation would be the one to succeed in sending a man into space. The United States and the Soviet Union each vied to be the first. They were deadly adversaries, and each had the power to start an atomic war. Previously, the first nation to cross the frontier would claim the prize of new territory. Because of its vast size, it was tougher to do this with the frontier of outer space. But still, the nation that could get there first would have a tremendous technological advantage over the other.

It happened on October 4, 1957. The Soviet Union successfully launched Sputnik 1, a 184-pound (83-kilogram) spherical satellite. The satellite orbited Earth every 95 minutes from an altitude as high as 560 miles (900 kilometers). The Russians were ahead.

The Soviet Union repeated its triumph one month later on November 3, 1957, with Sputnik 2. This satellite weighed 1,120 pounds (508 kilograms) and carried a live passenger—Laika, a small dog. The dog lived for several days in space and was put to sleep before oxygen and food supplies ran out.

The third satellite launch began to even the score. The United States launched its Explorer 1 satellite on January 31, 1958. Only 30 pounds (14 kilograms) in weight, the satellite carried scientific instruments whose data led to the discovery of radiation belts surrounding Earth.

The race for space was on. The real prize was to place humans in orbit. Before risking humans, however, both nations sent animals into space to see if they could survive there and if the rockets and space capsules each had constructed would work.

While the Soviet Union chose dogs for space flight, the United States chose to fly chimpanzees. Soviet scientists had used dogs for research for many years and it was natural for them to continue using them. U.S. scientists chose chimpanzees because physiologically chimps and humans are similar. Chimps could also be trained to perform tasks and this could verify if humans could work in space.

The first American "astrochimp" was a freckle-faced three-year-old male named Ham. Ham rode inside a bell-shaped space capsule of the same design that humans would ride in later. It was mounted on the top of a 58-foot (18-meter)-tall Redstone missile. The 16.5-minute flight was fraught with problems, not the least of which was a malfunctioning thrust regulator that resulted in Ham's capsule splashing in the Atlantic Ocean 120 miles (193 kilometers) farther downrange than planned. The capsule, slowly filling with water, was eventually plucked out of the ocean by a recovery helicopter and Ham was brought home safely.

The time to launch humans into space came, and again the Soviet Union led the way. On April 12, 1961, cosmonaut Yuri Gagarin rode Vostok I into space and orbited Earth one time before parachuting safely to Earth to a hero's welcome. Next came Alan B. Shepard Jr.'s turn. The American astronaut rocketed into space on May 5, 1961, and safely splashed down in the Atlantic Ocean 15.5 minutes later. Shepard's flight was virtually repeated by Virgil I. "Gus" Grissom on July 21, 1961. Although important to America's exploration of space, their flights seemed small and insignificant compared to the next Soviet space spectacular. On August 6, 1961, cosmonaut Gherman Titov orbited Earth 17 times and remained in space a full day!

There was one more important step U.S. rocket scientists felt was necessary before risking a flight to send a human astronaut into orbit. Using an Atlas missile, a more powerful booster than a Redstone, the four-year-old, 40-pound (18-kilogram) chimpanzee named Enos reached orbit and remained there for two trips around Earth on November 29, 1961. Enos, like Ham, had jobs to perform in space. Unfortunately, a malfunction occurred in the automatic systems, and when he did a job correctly, he was mistakenly given a mild electric shock to his feet instead of banana pellets for a reward. Enos's safe return convinced American scientists that it was time for an orbital flight with a human astronaut on board. It would be a dangerous mission.

Although Enos made it back safely, the Atlas rocket he rode on was temperamental and subject to many kinds of catastrophic failure. The Atlas weighed 260,000 pounds (118,000 kilograms) at launch, and most of that weight was highly explosive rocket fuel. The person picked to ride the Mercury Atlas to orbit was astronaut John H. Glenn Jr.

COUNTDOWN
COUNTDOWN
COUNTDOWN

CHAPTER 1
COUNTDOWN

The race to be first in space led the United States to create the National Aeronautics and Space Administration (NASA) in October 1958. At that time the president was Dwight D. Eisenhower. Eisenhower wanted NASA to be a civilian agency so that it could demonstrate to the world that U.S. efforts to conquer outer space were peaceful.

Almost immediately, NASA set about recruiting "astronauts" to fly into space. What kind of person would be needed? First thoughts went to the brave-hearted people who engaged in dangerous activities such as parachuting and mountain climbing. Later, it was decided that astronauts should be people who had worked in hazardous professions and functioned in difficult environments without succumbing to high levels of stress. Among the good candidates were test pilots and Arctic and Antarctic explorers. Before anyone could be recruited, however, Eisenhower decided that it would be better just to select astronauts from the pool of test pilots in the U.S. military.

After deciding on qualifications such as the minimum number of flying hours, age, height, and weight, the records of a group of 110 pilots were pulled from military files. The first astronaut corps would be chosen from this group.

The group of 110 didn't remain that size for long. Some pilots didn't like the idea of following a monkey into orbit, and the future astronauts were called "Spam in the can" by some pilots because the astronauts would only be passengers in their space capsule. By the following March, the number of astronaut candidates had dropped to 32.

Narrowing the field further meant long hours of interviews and batteries of unpleasant medical tests. NASA doctors had no idea what it would be like to be in space and so they tested for everything. The candidates were subjected to centrifuge tests where they were whirled around at high speed to simulate the stress of a rocket launch. They were locked in dark, soundproof rooms for many hours to see their reactions to confinement in a space capsule. They were placed in sound chambers where loud noises literally made their entire bodies shake. Ice water was poured into their ears for balance tests, and they were put in heated chambers to study how well they coped with high body temperatures.

On April 9, 1959, NASA announced the selection. Seven astronauts were picked for the first American manned space flights. The seven were M. "Scott" Carpenter, Virgil "Gus" Grissom Jr., Walter Schirra Jr., Leroy "Gordon" Cooper

The original seven astronauts were photographed in 1961 beside a Convair 106-B aircraft. They are (l. to r.) M. Scott Carpenter, L. Gordon Cooper Jr., John H. Glenn Jr., Virgil I. Grissom Jr., Walter M. Schirra Jr., Alan B. Shepard Jr., and Donald K. Slayton.

Jr., Alan Shepard Jr., Donald "Deke" Slayton, and John H. Glenn Jr. Their ages ranged from thirty-two to thirty-seven. Glenn was the oldest.

There would be seven manned spaceflights in a program NASA called "Mercury." The program was named after the wing-footed messenger of the Greek gods and the protector of travelers. The Mercury program had three main objectives—to place a manned spacecraft in orbit around Earth, to investigate the capabilities of a man in orbit, and to recover the man and spacecraft safely.

After the public unveiling, the seven astronauts began intensive training for their missions. They flew high-performance aircraft to keep up their piloting skills. They studied the designs for their space capsule and how to monitor and control its systems. They went through fittings for their space suits. They practiced water survival skills, since the Mercury capsules were designed to land in the ocean. Just in case, they also practiced wilderness survival skills on the chance that their capsule would go off course and they would land in a remote location such as a desert.

In addition to training, each astronaut was given special jobs to help advance the program. Cooper worked with the rocket scientists to ready the Redstone missile that would be used for the first three flights. Glenn worked on the Mercury capsule instrument panel. Carpenter worked on communications, Grissom worked on the hand controls and autopilot system, Shepard worked on recovery plans, Schirra worked on environmental systems and the flight suit, and Slayton worked on the Atlas rocket that would be used for the last four flights.

The work was exhausting and sometimes discouraging. Nothing NASA and the astronauts were attempting to do had ever been done before, and there was also the urgency of trying to beat the Russians into space. Furthermore, the

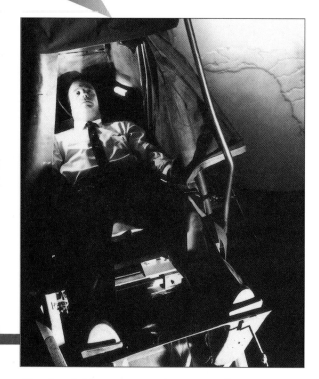

Project Mercury astronaut Scott Carpenter practiced controlling a spacecraft manually. The 1961 trainer allowed him to see an image of the Earth's surface at his feet as he worked the controls.

rockets that were going to carry each astronaut into space were unreliable. Faulty wiring, guidance malfunctions, and structural failures led to destroyed vehicles.

One test was especially frustrating. On November 21, 1960, a month and a half after Gagarin's successful orbital flight, a Mercury Redstone rocket ignited. The test was going to demonstrate to the rocket scientists, government leaders, and the American people that NASA was ready to catch up with the Russians. It was an unmanned suborbital test. The Redstone fired on cue but quickly shut down after lifting off only 1 inch (2.5 centimeters) from the pad. The capsule escape rocket fired next but left the capsule behind. The last insult took place when the capsule parachute popped out and hung limply alongside the rocket.

The Redstone failure was embarrassing, but there wasn't any time to dwell on it. Finally, NASA seemed to solve the problems with the Redstone. A Mercury Redstone rocket launch on December 19, 1960, lofted the capsule 130 miles (209 kilometers) into space and plopped it into the ocean 225 miles (362 kilometers) downrange of the Florida launch site. On January 31, 1961, the 37-pound (17-kilogram) chimpanzee named Ham safely flew to an altitude of 157 miles (253 kilometers) and landed 418 miles (673 kilometers) downrange. NASA was now ready to send up its first human astronaut. Alan Shepard was tapped for the flight. Before he could ride his Redstone into space the Soviet Union orbited cosmonaut Yuri Gagarin on April 12, 1961. It was a tremen-

Ham was rewarded with an apple after completing a ride in a Mercury capsule on January 31, 1961. Ham's adventure into space paved the way for human astronauts.

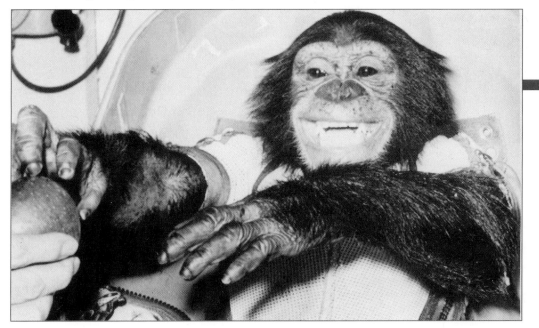

dous disappointment that the Russians got there first, but the U.S. space program moved forward anyway. Shepard reached space on May 5, 1961, in a near repeat of the chimpanzee's mission. His 15-minute, 22-second flight carried him to an altitude of 116.5 miles (187 kilometers) and 303 miles (488 kilometers) downrange.

Gus Grissom's flight followed the same trajectory a month and a half later. He splashed down only 3 miles (5 kilometers) from the recovery ship and was waiting for the helicopter to snare the capsule and place it on the deck. Suddenly, the side hatch blew open and Grissom could see water pouring into the capsule. He scrambled out of the capsule and began treading water. In his hurry to evacuate, Grissom neglected to close the oxygen inlet port on his space suit and it began filling with water. As his capsule sank beneath the waves, Grissom began swimming for his life until the helicopter plucked him out of the water and deposited him on the ship.

Next up for a Redstone mission was John Glenn. Before he could get to space the Russians put their second cosmonaut into orbit. Gherman Titov remained in space for an entire day. Before he returned, Titov completed 17 orbits "I have lived 17 days longer than each of you," he said. "For in 24 hours I have seen the Sun rise and set 17 times." Titov's flight and the success of Shepard and Grissom led NASA to scrap the third Redstone flight. The bigger and more powerful Atlas rocket would be used to place the first American in orbit. It was John H. Glenn Jr.'s turn to fly.

CHAPTER 2
A SHORT
4 HOURS,
55 MINUTES,
23 SECONDS

John Glenn awakened at 2:20 A.M. on February 20, 1962. He showered, got dressed, and had a breakfast of steak, eggs, toast, orange juice, and coffee. Doctors gave him a final physical exam and Glenn then put on his space suit. The suit was constructed of a silvery fabric consisting of aluminized nylon covering a layer of rubber-coated fabric. The inner layer would contain air to keep Glenn alive if the Mercury capsule lost its seal in space, letting out all the air inside. The suit was completed with boots that had to be laced up, gloves, and a helmet with a visor that could be opened and slipped over the head. The Mercury suit was designed to be worn unpressurized, although oxygen would flow through it to keep the astronaut inside cool and carry away perspiration. Beneath the suit, Glenn wore long underwear.

Two and a half hours later, Glenn arrived at Pad 14 at the Florida Cape Canaveral launch complex. After a short elevator ride, Glenn, with help from technicians, slid through the entry hatch and sat in his contoured launch seat. Written on the side of the Mercury capsule was the name *Friendship 7*. The *7* referred to the seven Mercury astronauts.

Glenn was assisted by technicians as he entered the Mercury capsule. The room they are in was located at the top of the gantry that surrounded the Atlas rocket.

Glenn's trip into space was to have taken place the previous December, and then it was to be in January. Mechanical problems like fuel leaks and bad weather that plagued the Cape led to one launch delay after another.

The Atlas rocket Glenn was perched on was a silver-colored metal cylinder that stood 68 feet (21 meters) tall. The stainless steel walls of the rocket were so thin (thinner than the thickness of a dime) that the only way the Atlas could support its own weight was for it to be pressurized. Pressure gave it strength just as air pressure inside a balloon makes it firm.

The upper end of the Atlas was tapered to meet the 6-foot (2-meter) diameter of the Mercury space capsule that sat on top. At the other end were its three rocket engines. Most of the 284,124-pound (128,877-kilogram) weight of the Atlas was the liquid oxygen and kerosene rocket fuel that would carry the Mercury capsule with Glenn inside into orbit. The Atlas began service as a military intercontinental ballistic missile. Only after the successful orbital flight of the chimpanzee Enos did NASA think the Atlas was safe enough for a human. As with the Redstone flights for Shepard and Grissom, a monkey had also led the way into space for Glenn.

Early in the design of the Mercury capsule the seven astronauts who would ride it joked that it was so small that "you don't climb into the Mercury spacecraft. You put it on." Scott Carpenter described the difficulty of getting into the capsule by saying, "You squeeze past all the gear that is mounted inside, like a man sliding under a bed. Once inside, you almost feel like just one more piece of machinery—the most important piece, of course."

The Mercury capsule looked something like a bell. It was more properly described as a truncated cone. That meant it was cone-shaped, but the point of the cone had been squared off. The bottom of the cone was slightly rounded. The idea of the rounded shape was to permit the capsule a safe reentry through Earth's atmosphere. It was covered with a heat shield material that would burn off, carrying away the heat, while the upper end of the cone was protected by being out of the heated airstream.

At launch, the 9.5-foot (3-meter)-high, 6-foot (2-meter)-wide capsule weighed 4,200 pounds (1,905 kilograms). On top of its truncated cone was a 16-foot (5-meter)-tall escape tower. Small but powerful rockets at the top of the tower could be used in the event of an emergency to thrust the Mercury capsule away from the Atlas if the Atlas were to go astray.

As John Glenn sat in his Mercury capsule, launch technicians began sealing his entryway hatch. Seventy bolts had to be tightened. While wrenching them all securely, the technicians noticed one of the bolts had broken, and the hatch had to be completely removed and repaired. While waiting for the job to be completed, Glenn looked through the capsule's periscope and was relieved to see that the bad weather at the Cape was breaking up. Then NASA patched in a telephone call to Glenn from his wife, Annie. During their marriage, Annie had supported him in his many endeavors as a marine corps aviator, a Korean War pilot, and a test pilot. Glenn's space flight would be his most dangerous endeavor yet, but the conversation seemed casual, and neither acknowledged the fact that Glenn could die in the next few hours. Glenn said to her, "Well, I'm going to the corner store to buy some chewing gum." It was a family joke, something he said when he was off on an adventure. Annie replied, "Well, don't take too long."

The countdown continued. With the hatch closed and all technicians clear of the pad, John Glenn was very alone. There was always the radio chatter in his headset and he could talk to launch control whenever he wanted. Still, he was alone and would be going into space by himself. Glenn studied the small instrument panels he had helped to design and reviewed the actions he would have to perform in flight.

Finally, there were no more delays. The countdown reached zero. At 9:47 A.M. the powerful Atlas rocket engines fired into life. The thunderous noise rumbled up the rocket, shaking Glenn so that it was difficult to focus on his instruments. He radioed mission control. "The clock is operating, we're underway."

Large billowing white clouds of smoke began enveloping the concrete launchpad with the red-painted steel gantry structure. The Atlas began its climb. Long orange flames lashed out from the three engines. Mission control responded to Glenn, "Reading you loud and clear."

Glenn replied, "Roger. OK, a little bumpy long about here." The Atlas was experiencing maximum dynamic pressure, or "max Q," as it rammed its way through the sound barrier. The spacecraft was shaking violently. Moments later, the Atlas was traveling faster than the speed of sound and the ride smoothed out. Glenn was on his way into space.

John Glenn was
riding in the black
Mercury capsule at
the top of the huge
Atlas rocket as it
lifted off from Cape
Canaveral.

The trip into space lasted only a few minutes. The acceleration of the rocket upward strained heavily on Glenn, making him feel six times heavier than normal. Finally, the Atlas used up its fuel. Explosive bolts fired and released the Mercury capsule from the Atlas. Small engines propelled the capsule away from the Atlas. When the engines stopped firing, the feeling of acceleration left Glenn. He radioed, "Zero G and I feel fine." John Glenn was orbiting Earth, and he felt as though he had no weight at all!

The Atlas rocket had performed wonderfully. It pitched the Mercury capsule into a slightly egg-shaped orbit that sped over Earth from as high as 162 miles (261 kilometers) and as low as 141 miles (227 kilometers). It was traveling at a speed of 17,541 miles (28,229 kilometers) per hour. Every second, Glenn traveled 5 miles (8 kilometers).

Mission control reported to Glenn that his spacecraft was on a path that could permit him to go for seven orbits. The plan was not to orbit seven times but to orbit three times. It was just good to know that the flight trajectory and speed were sufficient to complete the three planned orbits with room left over.

The automatic control system of the Mercury fired small control jets that turned the capsule around. Glenn got a view of the Atlantic Ocean and the falling Atlas rocket. "The capsule is turning around," Glenn reported. "Oh, that view is tremendous."

Now in orbit, Glenn could relax a bit. He loosened his harness to be more comfortable. Space flight doctors on

Earth listened to Glenn's every word. They wanted to know how easy it was to function in space, how he felt, how his heart was reacting. "This is very comfortable at zero G. I have nothing but very fine feeling. It just feels very normal and very good." A sensor for a heart monitor was taped to Glenn's chest. The heart rate was normal.

The major objectives of the *Friendship 7* flight were to see if it could be done and if the astronaut could do work in space. Glenn had a list of small tasks to perform as he shot around Earth. He had to tug on a rubber bungee cord to stimulate his heartbeat. He had to read an eye chart. He shook his head from side to side violently to see if he would be nauseated. "I have no ill effects at all from zero G." He reported his vision was excellent and had no feelings of nausea.

Glenn's view of Earth continued to be excellent. When he passed over Australia, it was nighttime. The sky was very black and he reported that he could see stars but not yet make out constellations. Residents from the town of Perth turned on their lights so that Glenn could see them from space. He spotted the lights and said they "show up very well." Then he asked mission control to call Perth and thank everybody for turning on the lights.

Glenn was circling Earth every 90 minutes. He saw a sunset and a sunrise only 45 minutes apart. As the Sun began climbing above the horizon, Glenn noticed thousands of tiny flecks surrounding his Mercury capsule. He called the flecks "fireflies." As the Sun got higher the flecks seemed to disappear, but they reappeared again at the same time for

This photograph of Earth from space was taken by Glenn during his historic first mission.

**An onboard camera cap-
tured John Glenn during
his first space flight.**

the second and third orbits. It was learned on a later mission
that the fireflies were small ice crystals that had come loose
from the side of the capsule and were traveling with him in
orbit.

Glenn continued his experiments and observations of
Earth. At one point he flipped up his face shield and squirted
applesauce from an aluminum toothpaste tube into his mouth.
The applesauce didn't taste very good, but he had no problem
swallowing it. Eating in space wasn't required for the short
time Glenn expected to be in orbit, but it would be for longer
missions. Scientists wanted to know if he could swallow.

At the end of Glenn's first orbit of Earth, the automatic
control system for his Mercury space capsule faltered. The
jets stopped on one side, started again, and then stopped on

the other side. The capsule began a slow turn. Glenn tried turning the system off and on again to restart it. The system was wasting fuel he would need for controlling the capsule on reentry, so he took over manual control of the system. Now that Glenn was flying the capsule, nobody any longer could claim that astronauts were just "Spam in the can."

While Glenn was controlling the Mercury, another problem cropped up. One of the mission controllers on Earth spotted a signal that indicated a possible problem with the Mercury capsule heat shield. It was a serious and potentially deadly problem. The only way Glenn could safely return to Earth was if his space capsule entered the atmosphere with its blunt end pointed downward. The heat shield on the capsule bottom might be coming loose.

The landing system for the Mercury capsule consisted of the heat shield and a heavy rubber landing bag. After entering the atmosphere and protecting the capsule, the shield was to have separated from the capsule bottom, stretching out the accordion-like landing bag. The bag, filled with air, would act as a shock absorber as the parachute dropped the capsule into the ocean.

The fear was that if the shield was coming loose, the rubber would be exposed to the tremendous heat of reentry and melt. The shield would drop off, exposing the capsule so that it would incinerate with Glenn inside.

There were two possibilities for the situation. One, the shield was loose. Two, the sensor that indicated the shield was loose was malfunctioning. If the second possibility was

the case, there would be no problem. Reentry would be safe. The trouble was that no one could be sure what was the real situation.

NASA engineers came up with a daring plan. Beneath the heat shield was a cluster of small rockets that Glenn would use to slow the Mercury capsule so that it could begin its descent from orbit. The engines were held to the bottom with straps that would separate and drop off the engines when their job was done. The plan was to leave the retrorockets attached, and perhaps the straps would help the shield to stay in place.

NASA decided not to tell Glenn what they thought might be happening. Radio messages to Glenn instructed him to confirm that the landing bag deploy switch was off. He figured something was going on, but he wasn't getting the whole story.

Soon it was time to reenter the atmosphere. About five minutes before firing the retrorockets, Glenn heard "This is capcom, *Friendship 7.* We are recommending that you leave the retro package on through the entire reentry."

Glenn responded. "This is *Friendship 7.* What is the reason for this? Do you have any reason?"

"Not at this time," came the answer. "This is a judgment of Cape Flight."

Glenn followed orders but figured out the situation for himself. There was a problem with the heat shield. The landing bag may have started deploying. If so, there was a good chance that he was going to start feeling a lot of heat shortly and never live to make it to the ocean. Finally, NASA told Glenn what was suspected and the reentry began.

As the capsule lowered, Earth's thin atmosphere began tearing at its heat shield. The temperature quickly climbed to the thousands of degrees. A strap from the retro-rocket pack tore off and slapped the window before streaming away burning. Thinking the entire pack had fallen off, Glenn radioed, "Uh, this is *Friendship 7*, I think the pack just let go."

Glenn saw chunks of flaming debris streak by. More of the pack broke away. The hot air around the capsule became ionized, or electrically charged. As expected, it interfered with radio communications.

At capcom, Alan Shepard kept radioing, "*Friendship 7*, this is Cape. Do you read? Over." The call was repeated again and again.

Finally there was a response. The radio crackled with, "Loud and clear, how me?" The capsule had slowed enough so that the air was no longer becoming ionized, and radio communication was possible again.

"Roger," radioed Shepard, "reading you loud and clear. How you doing?"

"Oh, pretty good," Glenn replied. "My condition is good but that was a real fireball, boy. I had great chunks of that retropack breaking off all the way through."

The mission wasn't over yet. The capsule was wobbling as it fell. Then the drogue parachute popped out to slow the descent and smooth the ride. This was followed by the main parachute. Glenn radioed, "Chute looks good!"

Aboard the USS *Noa*, Glenn took a last look at the capsule that was his home in space for three orbits of Earth.

Glenn splashed down in the Atlantic Ocean only a mile from a navy destroyer, 4 hours, 55 minutes, and 23 seconds after he lifted off from Florida. The capsule bobbed in the ocean. The temperature inside the capsule had soared to over 100°F (38°C). Glenn was getting seasick. A winch operator from the USS *Noa* plucked the capsule out of the water but accidentally banged it against the side of the destroyer before setting it on the deck.

Glenn was supposed to climb out through the top hatch of the capsule, but the heat, nausea, and the banging was enough. He radioed the crew to stand back and then yanked the emergency lever that set off small explosives that blew the side hatch out. John H. Glenn Jr. was safe. The first orbital Mercury mission was a success. Later examination of the Mercury capsule led to the conclusion that the heat shield indicator was faulty, and Glenn was never in any danger of the shield coming loose prematurely.

CHAPTER 3
A SECOND CHANCE

John H. Glenn Jr. returned home to find his personal world turned upside down. He was no longer just one of the seven Mercury astronauts. Glenn was the American who orbited Earth and put the United States back into the race for space. Although Gherman Titov spent a whole day in space, his flight, like Gagarin's, was conducted in secrecy, and the world only learned of the feats after success had been achieved. Glenn's accomplishment was done in the open for the world to see.

Glenn was honored in just about every way imaginable. There were parades, medals, speeches, schools named after him, and thousands upon thousands of handshakes and autographs. He and his wife got to meet President John F. Kennedy and a friendship blossomed. Vice President Lyndon B. Johnson rode with the Glenns in a New York ticker-tape

In a parade in Cocoa Beach, Florida, honoring him, Glenn was joined by President John F. Kennedy.

parade. Then Glenn got to address a joint session of the U.S. Congress. He was also invited to sign the National Geographic Society's Fliers' and Explorers' globe. Only a few other men, like Charles A. Lindbergh, had been invited to sign it.

For the first year after his historic flight, Glenn badgered NASA managers to be put back into the rotation for another space flight. A short time after Alan Shepard's flight, President Kennedy declared that the United States should send a man to the Moon and return him safely before the end of the decade. It was a terribly ambitious challenge, and it would have to be accomplished in less than nine years. The space program was changing rapidly and Glenn wanted to be there. There would be many flights that Glenn was qualified to fly. Following three more Mercury flights came the Gemini program. The Gemini space capsules would carry two astronauts into space. This would be followed with the three-man Apollo program that would set a man on the Moon.

At first, NASA managers would only tell Glenn that it would be best to wait. There were too many things for Glenn to do at the moment, and a decision to put him back into space would come later.

Glenn became more insistent and was finally told that NASA headquarters did not want Glenn to undertake another mission. Instead, they wanted Glenn to take management training to help lead the program from the ground. It was years later that he learned the real reason. President Kennedy had made the decision. Glenn was too valuable a symbol to risk on another space flight.

John H. Glenn Jr. resigned from NASA and from the marine corps. In 1964 he announced his candidacy to run in the Democratic primary election for senator of his home state of Ohio. He might have had a good chance of winning but fate took over. While taking a shower, Glenn slipped and injured his head in the fall. A lengthy hospital stay made him physically unable to campaign for office and he withdrew from the race.

In the years that followed, Glenn recovered from his head injury and entered into business. He ran for office again in 1970 but lost in the primary election to Cleveland business-man Howard Metzenbaum. Metzenbaum eventually lost the election to the Republican candidate.

Glenn began a period of investing in hotels and eventually became a wealthy man. Again he campaigned for the U.S. Senate, and his persistence finally paid off. He was elected in 1974. Glenn became an effective and popular senator from Ohio, and he even began a run for the president's office in 1984 but withdrew from the race during the primaries because of a poor showing.

He continued to serve the citizens of Ohio as a U.S. senator, but he never gave up his dream to fly into space again. He had now reached his seventies, and many would have thought him too old to return to space. As a matter of fact, following Glenn's 1962 space flight, he was considered by some NASA managers to be too old to fly again even then.

For Glenn, being an old man was the perfect reason for another trip into space. He got the idea in 1995 while reading a scientific study that compared the effects of being in space to growing older. In Earth's orbit, where it feels as though there is no gravity acting on an astronaut, significant changes take place in the human body. Scientists have identi-fied at least fifty of them. Some body fluids shift to the upper body, giving a puffy look to the face and neck. The legs thin out slightly in what is sometimes referred to as the "chicken legs" effect. The bones in the back spread out, causing astro-

In 1975, Senator John Glenn discussed various accomplishments with former Cleveland Indians great Bob Feller. Feller was inducted into the Baseball Hall of Fame in 1962. That was the same year that Glenn became the first American to orbit Earth.

nauts to temporarily grow taller. There are changes in the body's immune system, which fights diseases. Muscles get weaker, problems with balance occur, and bones lose some of their calcium. These changes and more mimic some of the effects of aging.

Glenn noticed something else important about space medical research. The only people studied in space usually were adults in their late thirties to early fifties. The oldest astronaut was sixty-one when he last flew. All were in excellent condition. Glenn knew that 35 million adults in the United States were sixty-five or older, and statistics pointed to 100 million senior citizens in the next fifty years. None of the astronauts flying in space represented these older citizens.

NASA, he believed, needed to fly an older person to begin direct research on the process of aging. Who best to represent senior citizens in space?—John H. Glenn Jr.

Glenn began a campaign to get himself assigned to a future space shuttle mission. He first talked to doctors and scientists who specialized in aging and began amassing a wealth of scientific studies on past research and questions his return to space might be able to answer. When he was ready with reports in hand, Glenn approached NASA. NASA took his request seriously and ordered a variety of medical tests on Glenn to see if there were any special risks to sending him into space. Glenn passed all the tests and won the recommendations of the doctors who had examined him. His proposed flight also won support from the National Institute of Health and the National Institute on Aging. NASA finally agreed.

On January 16, 1998, NASA Administrator Daniel S. Goldin held a press conference. He announced to the world that John Glenn would fly in space on the STS-95 space shuttle *Discovery* mission set for October. "Not only is John Glenn a marine test pilot, an astronaut, and the first American to orbit Earth," Goldin said, "[but] he brings a unique blend of experience to NASA. He has flight, operational, and policy experience. Unlike most astronauts, he never got the opportunity for a second flight. He is part of the NASA family, an American hero, and he has the right stuff for this mission." John Glenn, at seventy-seven years of age, was going to return to space.

CHAPTER 4
GETTING READY

There are several kinds of astronauts who fly into space. Pilot astronauts are people who were high-performance aircraft test pilots before qualifying for astronaut training. The pilots fly the space shuttle. On each mission, one pilot astronaut is designated as the commander and is in charge of the entire mission. A second pilot astronaut also flies. Rather than call the second pilot the copilot, this astronaut is simply called the pilot. The commander is the most experienced flyer on the mission and sits in the left front seat of the space shuttle orbiter. The pilot is less experienced but will eventually be assigned as the commander on a future mission. The pilot sits in the right seat. On John Glenn's STS-95 mission, the commander would be Curtis L. Brown. This would be Brown's fifth flight into space. The pilot would be Stephen W. Lindsey, and STS-95 would be his second flight.

A second category of astronaut is the mission special-ist. Mission specialist astronauts are scientists, doctors, and

engineers who have advanced college degrees and have had several years' experience doing research or engineering. Their function in space is to conduct scientific experiments, operate the large mechanical arm in the orbiter's payload bay, and do space walks if needed. On STS-95, there were three mission specialists. Scott Parazynski was a medical doctor and had flown in space twice before. With him was Stephen K. Robinson. Robinson was a research scientist in aerodynamics and computer visualization. STS-95 would be his second flight. The third mission specialist was Pedro Duque from Spain. Duque, an aeronautical engineer, was an astronaut from the European Space Agency. STS-95 would be his first flight.

The third category of astronaut is the payload specialist. Payload specialists are usually one-time astronauts who fly in space to conduct a specific piece of research in an area in which they are the most qualified. Chiaki Mukai, a medical doctor from the Japanese Space Agency, was assigned to the STS-95 mission because of her medical and scientific research experience. She had flown in space once before.

The last member of the STS-95 crew was John H. Glenn Jr. He too was flying for his second time. The first time he flew he was a pilot astronaut. This time, Glenn was a payload specialist. His primary area of emphasis would be medical studies on himself.

Training for an astronaut is an exhausting process for a young person and much more so for a person seventy-seven

This photo shows the astronauts who were part of John Glenn's second space mission. Standing (l. to r.): Scott Parazynski, Steve Robinson, Chiaki Mukai, Pedro Duque, John Glenn. Sitting (l. to r.): Steve Lindsay, Curt Brown.

years old. Glenn reported to the NASA Johnson Space Center in Houston, Texas, for months of classroom study, equipment and vehicle familiarization training, space flight simulations, fittings for his launch and entry suit, training on

John Glenn practices using one of the cameras for the flight. He is sitting on the flight deck of a crew compartment trainer, a simulator that replicates *Discovery*'s controls.

how to conduct the experiments and other duties assigned to him, and survival training.

Practically the whole of the Johnson Space Center is designed either to control missions in space or to simulate them for the astronauts who will soon be traveling to space. There are crew compartment trainers that look and work like the crew cabins of the space shuttle orbiter except that they remain on the ground. Inside, the crew is taught where everything is. For Glenn, this was an unusual experience. His Mercury capsule had been very different, and Glenn wasn't used to all that room to move around in.

The space shuttle *Discovery*, in which Glenn would ride, is 122 feet (37.2 meters) long. *Freedom 7*, Glenn's Mercury capsule, was only 9.5 feet (2.9 meters) high and 6 feet (1.8 meters) wide. The shuttle's orbiter payload bay is so large that two dozen Mercury capsules could be stuffed inside! The Mercury capsule was also a lightweight in comparison. At liftoff, it weighed just over 2.1 tons (1,930 kilograms), whereas *Discovery* at liftoff, with nothing in its payload bay, would weigh 76.9 tons (69,772 kilograms).

There are many other differences between *Freedom 7* and *Discovery*. *Freedom 7* gave Glenn only 36 cubic feet (1 cubic meter) of living space. *Discovery*, on the other hand, has 2,325 cubic feet (65.8 cubic meters) of living space. Of course, *Discovery* would be holding a crew of seven but still, divided equally, each crew member would have almost ten times the space that Glenn had in *Freedom 7*. As a matter of fact, *Discovery* could hold 64 persons if they were packed in as tight as Glenn had been during his first flight.

Another big difference is that *Discovery* has two decks. The flight deck is where the commander, pilot, Parazynski, and Duque would sit. Robinson, Mukai, and Glenn would sit in seats on the middeck located below the flight deck. After reaching orbit all seats but the commander's and pilot's would be folded up and put away to make more room.

The flight deck of *Discovery* is divided into halves. The forward section is where the flying controls are located. *Freedom 7* had only 64 switches and 19 dials and other status displays. *Discovery*'s flight deck features 1,075 switches and 559 dials and status displays. The aft section of the flight deck holds the controls for the payload bay, including the controls for the 50-foot (15.2-meter)-long robot arm. With Glenn stuck in his seat for the entire Mercury flight, his capsule only had one deck, and all controls were right in front of his face.

Three more things make *Discovery* different from *Freedom 7*. *Discovery* has a galley for preparing hot and cold food. There would be a wide choice of foods available for the flight, and they would taste much better than applesauce

Glenn (center) participated in a food-tasting session at the Johnson Space Center. He was joined by payload specialist Chiaki Mukai (l.) and Curtis Brown, mission commander.

from an aluminum toothpaste tube. There are sleeping bunks with sliding doors for a good night's rest. Glenn did not have time to sleep during his first mission, but later Mercury astronauts slept in their seats. Finally, and most important, *Discovery* has a lavatory. In the microgravity of space, a good working lavatory is essential on extended flights, not only for sanitary conditions but also for crew morale. The toilet on *Discovery* is located just inside the entry hatch on the mid-deck. A door can be opened and curtains erected for privacy. Astronauts urinate into a tube that has a vacuum suction to keep the urine from floating back out. Solid waste is collected in a high-tech space version of a pit toilet. Again, a slight vacuum keeps the waste where it should be. In contrast, Glenn had a tube and a pouch for urination inside his space suit on *Freedom 7*.

An important difference in the *Discovery* flight is how long it would remain in space. Glenn's Mercury flight lasted only 4 hours, 55 minutes, and 23 seconds from liftoff to splashdown. *Discovery*'s flight would last nearly nine days. During his first flight in space, Glenn didn't have much time for research. He got to take some pictures of Earth, try eating applesauce, and measure his blood pressure, but most of his time was taken up with controlling *Freedom 7* when the autopilot system began acting up.

Discovery's mission would be packed with experiments and other tasks. A special commercially built module called Spacehab would be placed in the forward section of *Discovery*'s payload bay, and the crew could access it through the air-lock door that connects the middeck and the payload bay. Spacehab would be filled with experiments sponsored by the Japanese Space Agency and the European Space Agency.

Also located in the payload bay would be the Spartan 201 free-flying satellite. Spartan 201s have been flown several times. They are picked up from the payload bay with the shuttle's mechanical arm and released in space above the orbiter. As the orbiter is moved away to do other things, the Spartan conducts scientific research. On this mission, the

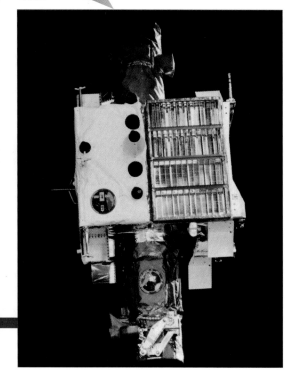

The STS-95 crew released this Spartan 201 satellite early in the flight and retrieved it after it had monitored the solar wind and the Sun's corona.

Spartan 201 would study the Sun's atmosphere for about 40 hours before being retrieved by the shuttle and returned to its berth in the payload bay.

The payload bay would also carry a few instruments for astronomy studies and several small experiments in processing materials in the microgravity of space. Additional cargo would be a small U.S. Navy communications satellite called PANSAT (Petite Amateur Navy Satellite) that was constructed by the Naval Postgraduate School. PANSAT would be kicked out of the payload bay using springs during the mission and left in orbit.

For John Glenn, the STS-95 experiments would be exhausting. As the chief guinea pig of the flight, he expected to be poked and prodded constantly. He would donate blood, monitor his body temperature, participate in sleep pattern studies, and study balance, just to name a few. To make this happen, Glenn would be attached to as many as twenty-one probes during parts of his mission and would swallow a radio transmitter capsule to measure his core body temperature.

Glenn had to learn how to conduct all of the experiments he was assigned to do, and that meant working with the scientists and doctors who designed the experiments. It meant spending long hours studying manuals and learning procedures. Glenn also had to learn how to use the shuttle's toilet and galley. He had to experience again the feel of a launch. One way to do this was to ride a motion-based simulator of the orbiter. The simulator was a replica of the flight deck and was mounted on hydraulic cylinders. The commander and pilot would practice launch and landing procedures over and over again. The other crew members rode in the backseats to feel the vibrations of a shuttle liftoff. Except for the G forces, the simulator gives a realistic experience. Test conductors outside the simulator monitor the simulation and occasionally throw in malfunctions for the crew to handle. Sometimes the vehicle crashes, but the crew learns from their mistakes.

Glenn didn't miss out on the G forces entirely. He was taken to a centrifuge at Brooks Air Force Base in San Antonio, Texas. There, he was whirled around in a machine that simulated 3 Gs. Glenn weighed three times normal in the centrifuge, but he felt no ill effects. After all, he had felt more than twice the G force during the flight of *Freedom 7*.

Then there were the emergency procedures to learn. Glenn had to learn how to bail out of the orbiter while it was in flight. No one has ever had to do that, but every crew member had to know how to do it. In another safety training exercise, parachute straps suspended Glenn over a

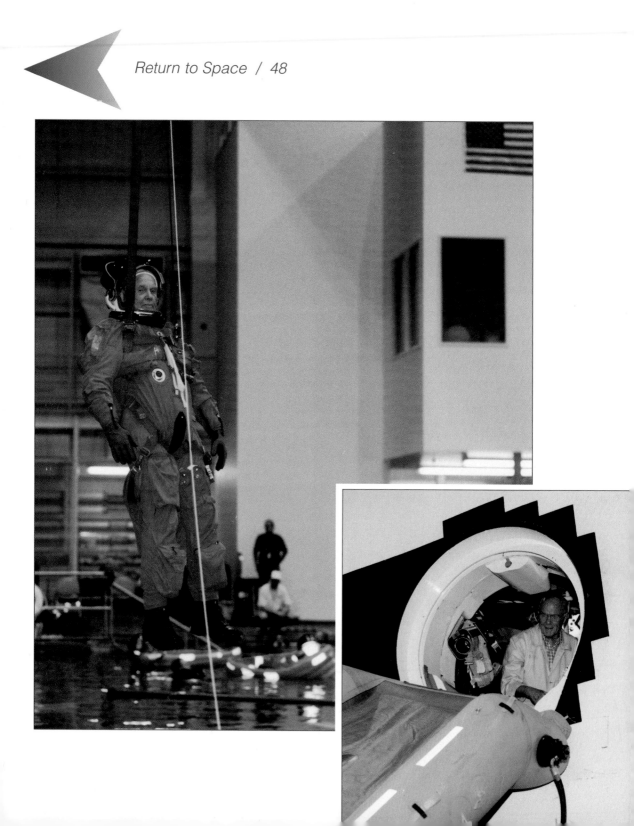

6.2-million-gallon (23.4-million-liter) water tank. He wore the bright orange "pumpkin suit" all shuttle astronauts wear during launch and landing. If the crew did have to abandon the shuttle and parachute to safety, they might land in water. They needed to know what to do. Suddenly, the straps let go and Glenn was plopped into the tank. He momentarily sank beneath the surface, and then automatic life preservers popped him back up like an empty soft-drink bottle. A life raft automatically inflated and Glenn had to struggle to get into it. The struggle was exhausting even for a younger person. Glenn made it.

Glenn also had to learn how to reel himself out of the orbiter to the ground on a wire during an emergency evacuation and how to slide down an inflatable chute. The most important safety lesson Glenn and his crewmates would learn was how to function as a team. There was much to know, but this was the price of space flight.

Astronauts have to develop water survival skills. Glenn is about to be dumped into a 6.2-million-gallon tank of water so he can practice scrambling into an inflatable life raft. In the event of an emergency evacuation while the orbiter is on the ground, an escape slide (bottom) would inflate.

CHAPTER 5

A LONG
213 HOURS,
44 MINUTES,
56 SECONDS

Powerful floodlights bathing the space shuttle *Discovery* were shut off as the Sun rose over the Atlantic Ocean to the east on the morning of October 29, 1998. As the sky brightened, *Discovery* seemed to glow in its own light. The delta-winged orbiter stood upright. Behind it was the giant external tank containing 721,000 pounds (327,046 kilograms) of liquid oxygen and 1.6 million pounds (725,760 kilograms) of hydrogen. The tank was covered with a thick layer of foam insulation to keep the liquid gases inside super cold. The insulation had turned brownish in the days it had been exposed to the sunlight on the launchpad. Attached to the right and left sides of the tank were the two torpedo-shaped white solid rocket boosters. They are called "solid" because the propellant inside them is a solid.

Flanking the vehicle to the left was a gray steel support structure that had an arm with a small room attached pressed against the nose of the orbiter. All this was atop the large concrete mound of the launchpad.

The Sun continued to rise in a clear sky. It was going to be a perfect day to travel to space.

The crew of STS-95 had begun to get ready for liftoff. This time, for Glenn, there would not be months of delays. Space flight was still complicated, but NASA had the launch process down to a science and rarely were there long delays.

The crew rose, showered, and got dressed. There were final medical evaluations and breakfast. Glenn's meal was similar to the one he had before lifting off on *Freedom 7*. He had steak fillet, two eggs over easy, wheat toast, grits, and ketchup. There was a cake with a frosting version STS-95 mission patch decorating its top. The cake would not be eaten then. It would be frozen and saved for a celebration after landing. Lots of pictures were taken, and then it was time to suit up.

The STS-95 patch was designed by the crew.

The suits the crew of STS-95 donned were quite different from the space suit Glenn wore for *Freedom 7*. Glenn's *Freedom 7* suit was aluminized to help protect him from the heat of atmospheric reentry. It weighed 30 pounds (13.5 kilograms) and was designed to be worn for the entire flight. The Advanced Crew

Escape Suit (ACES) for shuttle astronauts was designed for launch and reentry only. At other times during the flight the crew could wear ordinary clothes. The outside of the ACES is bright orange so that the crew could easily be spotted if they bailed out from the orbiter as they glided in toward a landing. Cooling in the ACES is accomplished by running cool water through tubes laced through underwear each crew member wears. Beneath the cooling underwear, the crew members wear an adult version of a diaper.

The ACES weighs about 90 pounds (41 kilograms) because safety gear such as a parachute and a life raft are included in the back. Moving about on Earth while wearing an ACES is quite difficult and took lots of practice. It was especially difficult to get into the orbiter and into the launch seats when the orbiter was standing on its tail on the launchpad.

Once decked out in their suits, the crew marched outside to a throng of wellwishers and into a van for the 3.4-mile (5.5-kilometer) ride to the *Discovery* launchpad. An elevator carried them up 195 feet (60 meters) to the white room in the launch gantry. The room was mounted at the end of a swinging arm that held it next to *Discovery*'s entry hatch. One at a time, the crew boarded and technicians assisted them into their seats. Glenn sat in the middle seat on the middeck between Steve Robinson and Chiaki Mukai.

The launch was delayed briefly while flight controllers studied an alarm that rang during cabin leak checks. There was a further delay when several small tourist aircraft strayed into the launch area. Finally, everything was ready.

The backward-moving mission clock reached T minus 6 seconds, and *Discovery*'s three main engines began gulping thousands of gallons of liquid hydrogen and liquid oxygen. Flames belched into flame trenches while huge white steam clouds billowed upward. At 1:19 P.M. Central Standard Time, the clock reached zero. *Discovery*'s two solid rocket engines ignited and the clock started counting forward. Immediately, explosives shattered the nuts attached to hold-down bolts, and *Discovery* leaped into the air on more than 6.5 million pounds (29 million Newtons) of thrust. As it climbed skyward, bright pillars of orange flame streaked downward more than 600 feet (183 meters). Thunderous waves of sound rolled across the Florida landscape, engulfing the tens of thousands of cheering spectators. As with all space launches, the vehicle shook.

Discovery lifted off at 2:19 p.m. EST, October 29, 1998, on a nine-day mission in Earth orbit.

Two minutes after ignition, the boosters had consumed their fuel and dropped off to parachute into the ocean. *Discovery* continued its climb on the thrust of its three main engines. Less than nine minutes after liftoff, *Discovery* was well over the Atlantic Ocean and orbiting Earth. Forty-five minutes after launch, *Discovery*'s small orbital maneuvering system engines were fired to round off the orbit at a high point of 349 miles (562 kilometers) and a low point of 340 miles (547 kilometers). *Discovery* was orbiting Earth every 95 minutes and 54 seconds.

While sending space shuttle crews to orbit was pretty commonplace, John Glenn's presence attracted great interest. How would he feel in microgravity? His first flight 36 years before gave him 4 hours, 55 minutes, and 23 seconds of microgravity, and he was strapped down for the whole time. On *Discovery*, he could move about and doing so has caused many an astronaut to get space sick the first day or two in orbit. Three hours and ten minutes into the flight, Glenn radioed Earth for the first time.

"**H**ello, Houston. This is PS 2 (payload specialist 2) and they got me sprung out of the middeck for a little while. We are just going by Hawaii and that is absolutely gorgeous."

"Roger that. Glad you are enjoying the show," replied capcom.

Glenn replied, "Enjoying the show is right. This is

beautiful. The best part is … a trite old statement: zero G and I feel fine."

A little under two hours later, Commander Curt Brown pointed out that the STS-95 mission had surpassed Glenn's previous flight for time in orbit.

The first day in orbit was filled with powering up the experiments mounted in *Discovery*'s payload bay and setting up equipment needed for the 80-plus experiments that would be conducted inside. Bedtime came at 11:45 P.M. Glenn slipped into a bunk along one of the middeck walls and slid the door closed. Even though he was asleep, medical studies of Glenn were underway. A capsule that he swallowed radioed his inner body temperature to recording instruments.

For the next several days, the crew of STS-95 kept themselves very busy. The Petite Amateur Naval Satellite was released from the payload bay. Parazynski and Robinson unstowed the payload bay robot arm and checked out its motion in preparation for the release of the Spartan solar science satellite. Glenn activated some of the medical experiments. Since he was also the chief medical experiment subject, he had to provide 10 blood samples and 16 urine samples during the flight. Researchers needed the samples to look into the effects of space flight on his body. They wanted to know if the removal of gravity's effects changed Glenn's balance and perception, immune system responses, bone and muscle density, metabolism and blood flow, and sleep patterns. There was much to learn from the seventy-seven-year-old man.

**A view of
Discovery's
open cargo
bay**

On the first Saturday of the flight, Curt Brown and
John Glenn took time from their busy schedule to talk with
students in three locations across the United States. The students asked dozens of questions:

"Senator Glenn," asked students at the Center of
Science and Industry in Columbus, Ohio, "were you more
nervous being the first American to orbit the Earth or to be
the oldest man ever in space?"

"Well," Glenn replied, "I think they are both great things to participate in and I had a wonderful time the first time. I think I was probably more nervous back in those days because we did not know much about space flight in those days; we were sort of feeling our way and finding out what would happen to the human body in space…"

"Would microgravity lessen the effects of certain types of joint pain?" another student asked.

"I think it would because when you no longer have the same kind of pressure on those joints quite a lot of pain should be lessened. You know we are studying a lot of things up here…one of the experiments I started out on yesterday was OSTEO; it is an experiment that looks into bone structure…We hope to learn a lot that will benefit a lot of people on Earth."

At the Newseum in Arlington, Virginia, students wanted to know if NASA would ever study the effects of space flight on the young.

"Well, I think we will get around to that sometime. But you know you have to be careful because…for young people we would be talking about their bones being formed and their bodies changing very rapidly as part of the growth process and up here that might be interfered with rather drastically. So I think we have to be rather careful on that."

Curt Brown was asked by students at the John Glenn High School in New Concord, Ohio (Glenn's hometown), how it feels to work with such an American hero.

"When I was growing up," Brown said, "Senator Glenn was definitely one of my heroes. I was pretty young at that

time, but as we grew up [and read] the history books and the events of the times you understood how that all got started and Senator Glenn was a big part of that. How does it feel to work with Senator Glenn? Well, I think I speak for the whole crew, it has been our pleasure and we are honored to have him aboard. But he is one of the crew members and he has been very professional and energetic and motivated...he is a member of the crew and we are all teammates..."

The STS-95 mission continued on for seven more days. Unlike Glenn's *Freedom 7* flight, there were no major problems or suspected major problems. Except for a small leak in one of *Discovery's* small jets, the reaction control system that controls *Discovery's* direction in space did not malfunction. There was no faulty indicator to say there might be a problem with the landing system. There were a few problems—a small door that covered *Discovery's* drag chute fell off during liftoff, and a tiny water leak developed from a hose in a new system that filters iodine out of *Discovery's* drinking water—but these were minor difficulties easily gotten around.

Glenn faithfully conducted his medical studies and served as the mission's chief photographer for documenting the mission and experiment results. He continued to donate blood and began to joke about it. "Scott's [Parazynski] taken my blood so many times that when I see him I say, 'Here comes Dracula.'" At night, Glenn donned a weblike cap that pressed sensors to different parts of his head to monitor electrical activity while sleeping. On some days, Glenn attached electrodes to his chest to monitor and record his heart activity.

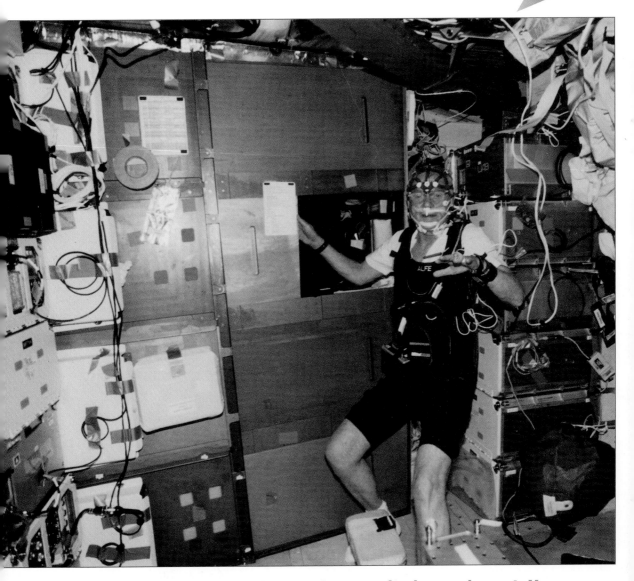

John Glenn was hooked up to sleep-monitoring equipment. Here he stands near his sleep station on the middeck of *Discovery*.

The other crew members each had their own exhausting schedule of jobs to do. One of Chiaki Mukai 's experiments was to study the effects of microgravity on oyster toadfish. Pedro Duque conducted plant-growing experiments. Steve Robinson successfully released the SPARTAN satellite for a two-day solar science mission. Curt Brown and Steve Lindsey maneuvered *Discovery* away from the satellite and then returned to it so that Robinson could capture it and return it to the payload bay.

On their second Saturday in space, the crew of STS-95 made their final preparations to return home. The doors of the payload bay had to be closed. All equipment had to be stowed in the lockers on the middeck and in Spacehab. The crew had to put on their ACES launch and entry suits again. They also drank lots of water. One of the adjustments the human body makes to space is that it tends to eliminate more water than usual. On reentry, this condition makes astronauts a bit light-headed. Drinking extra water before landing helps to counter that feeling. Glenn, like the rest of the crew, loaded up on water.

At the right moment, Commander Curt Brown and Pilot Steve Lindsey fired *Discovery*'s orbital maneuvering system engines to slow the vehicle. *Discovery*'s path changed from a circular orbit to a long, sloping glide that would end at the Kennedy Space Center in Florida a few miles from where it had taken off nine days before. Its bottom side slammed into Earth's upper atmosphere. Instead of burning off, *Discovery*'s heat shield insulated the crew from the intense heat generated during reentry.

Soon the air was thick enough for *Discovery*'s wings to start working like wings. It became a glider and headed for the 3-mile (5-kilometer)-long concrete runway at the Kennedy Space Center. As *Discovery* was nearing the runway, spectators heard a double sonic boom that all aircraft make when they are traveling faster than the speed of sound. *Discovery* slowed and made its final approach. About 330 feet (100 meters) above the runway its landing gear dropped down. The rear wheels touched first, and the nose pitched downward until the forward gear touched down as well. Small puffs

Space shuttle *Discovery* touched down on November 7, 1998, landing on orbit 135 after a successful mission.

of tire smoke appeared as *Discovery* began to slow. A small parachute and then a larger one popped out from the tail section, slowing it further. Finally the chutes were released and *Discovery* rolled to a stop.

A variety of support vehicles circled around the space travelers. Everybody waited for the crew to depart down the roll-up staircase. The wait was longer than usual. It was later learned that John Glenn was having a similar experience to his *Freedom 7* landing. Glenn was nauseated and began throwing up. He later said, "I preloaded with too much fluid coming down."

With Glenn feeling weak and unsteady, the crew appeared and came down the stairs to lots of congratulations. They then made the traditional walk around the outside of *Discovery*.

For John H. Glenn Jr., the STS-95 mission appeared to be over, but it wasn't. There would be more medical evaluations. It was important to compare his condition after flight with his condition before and during flight. Glenn got wired up again for sleep tests. He had to give more blood and urine samples. There would also be six months of muscle and bone tests. The researchers would not release the results of his work for at least a year after landing.

EPILOGUE

John Glenn's first flight into space lasted only a few hours as he orbited Earth just three times. Glenn demonstrated that the United States could place a man in Earth orbit and bring him back to Earth safely. When Glenn flew into space in 1962, he was only one of three persons to have orbited Earth. The other two were Soviet cosmonauts. Glenn got to see three sunrises and three sunsets, see the lights of Perth, Australia, see the world's oceans and continents, see clouds, and see stars. Glenn demonstrated that an astronaut could not only survive microgravity but also could do useful work in space.

John Glenn's second flight into space lasted nearly nine days, and he orbited Earth 135 times as he traveled 3.6 million miles (5.8 million kilometers). Glenn got to view the world again, and again see the lights of Perth. He had time to appreciate the view. "It's quite something," he said after the mission, "to look down on this blue planet, seeing that little film of air that surrounds it. You fly over the Mediterranean,

over the Middle East—and it's so beautiful. You wonder why in the world humans can't solve all the problems they've created and left to fester over the centuries." Glenn had time to conduct many experiments on this flight and to tell the people at home how he felt about returning to space. ".... yes, it was worth waiting for. Yes, it certainly was. Not just as a personal experience, but also in looking forward to some of the research we are going to do that is going to benefit everybody back there on Earth, benefit all of us into the future."

Glenn returned to space thirty-six years after his first flight to advance medical knowledge. In late January 2000, scientists reported that Glenn endured the effects of space flight as well as, if not better than, the younger astronauts on the mission. "The [test] results are inherently exciting because they challenge the concept of the elderly being frail individuals," said Dr. David Williams, director of the Life Sciences Center at the Johnson Space Center.

Glenn's flight may not lead to any great medical breakthroughs. We might not recognize any improvements in our lives because of his contributions. But certainly, his successful mission has changed our perception of the elderly.

Our next journeys will take us to the International Space Station that will be completed in Earth orbit in 2003 or 2004. From there, we can return to the Moon to stay and then travel to Mars. John Glenn will be there too because his contributions, like those of thousands of other people, showed us the way.

GLOSSARY

Advanced Crew Escape Suit (ACES) the orange "pumpkin" launch and reentry suit worn by space shuttle astronauts

Atlas the rocket that propelled John H. Glenn Jr. into space

capcom (capsule communicator) the astronaut who communicates directly from mission control to astronauts in space

Discovery the name of the space shuttle that carried John Glenn and six other astronauts on a nine-day mission in space, starting October 29, 1998

external tank the farm silolike propellant tank containing liquid hydrogen and liquid oxygen for the space shuttle's three main engines

Freedom 7 the name of the Mercury space capsule John H. Glenn Jr. rode into orbit in 1962

heat shield a layer of materials that protects a spacecraft from burning due to the heat of atmospheric friction during reentry

International Space Station an orbital platform for scientific study that is being constructed by many nations of the world

Mercury capsule the small, bell-shaped spacecraft used by Mercury astronauts

mission control a team of engineers and astronauts who assist the space shuttle crew in orbit

National Aeronautics and Space Administration (NASA) the agency of the U.S. government charged with exploring the atmosphere and outer space

orbit the path a spacecraft or satellite takes around Earth

orbiter the delta-winged orbital spacecraft portion of the space shuttle

Project Mercury the first manned space program of the United States

Redstone the rocket used to send the first two American astronauts into space

reentry the passage of an orbital spacecraft back into Earth's atmosphere

satellite a spacecraft that orbits a planet or moon

solid rocket boosters solid propellant rocket boosters attached to the external tank of the space shuttle

space shuttle the current space vehicle used by the National Aeronautics and Space Administration to carry astronauts into space

Spartan 201 a recoverable solar science satellite

JOHN H. GLENN JR.
CHRONOLOGY

1921 born in Cambridge, Ohio

1923 family relocates to New Concord, Ohio, where Glenn goes to school and much later earns a Bachelor of Science degree in Engineering from Muskingum College

1941 enlists in the U.S. Navy after Pearl Harbor is bombed

1942 becomes a marine aviator

1943 marries Annie Castor

1944 flies combat missions in the Pacific

1945 son, David, is born

1947 flies combat missions in China; daughter, Lyn, is born

1953 flies combat missions in Korea

1954 becomes a test pilot

1959 becomes a Mercury astronaut

1962 orbits Earth three times

1965 works for Royal Crown Cola

1974 elected U.S. senator from Ohio

1984 withdraws from race for Democratic presidential nomination

1992 elected for fourth and last term in U.S. Senate

1998 as payload specialist on STS-95 space shuttle mission becomes oldest astronaut to fly in space

1999 retires from the U.S. Senate to pursue new adventures

FOR MORE INFORMATION

Books:

Angel, Ann. *John Glenn, Space Pioneer.* New York: Fawcett Columbine, 1989.

Cole, Michael D. *John Glenn, Astronaut and Senator.* Hillside, NJ: Enslow Publishers, Inc., 1993.

Montgomery, Scott, and Timothy R. Gaffney. *Back in Orbit, John Glenn's Return to Space.* Atlanta, GA: Longstreet, 1998.

Magazine Articles:

Newcott, William R. "John Glenn: Man With a Mission." *National Geographic*, vol. 195, no. 6, 1999, pp. 60–81.

Voas, Robert B. "John Glenn's Three Orbits in *Friendship 7.*" *National Geographic*, vol. 158, no. 6, 1962, pp. 792–827.

NASA Internet Sites:

http://spaceflight.nasa.gov/shuttle/archives/index.html

http://www.ksc.gov/history/mercury/mercury.html

http://www.pbs.org/kcet/johnglenn/index2.htm

http://www.rtd1.com/glenn/index.html

INDEX